Golden Retrievers

Dog Books for Kids

By
K. Bennett and John Davidson

JD-Biz Publishing

All Rights Reserved.

No part of this publication may be reproduced in any form or by any means, including scanning, photocopying, or otherwise without prior written permission from JD-Biz Corp

Copyright © 2014. All Images Licensed by Fotolia and 123RF.

Read More Amazing Animal Books

Purchase at Amazon.com

Table of Contents

Introduction

Chapter 1 Early History

Chapter 2 Fascinating Features & Care

Chapter 3 Amazing Golden Retriever facts

Conclusion A Family's best friend

Author Bio

Introduction

"A dog is man's best friend, and vice versa."
-Anonymous

🐾 Golden Retrievers are considered 'the perfect family pet.' They are charming, warm, tolerant, versatile, intelligent, and very friendly. As a large size dog breed, they were originally bred as gun dogs and used during hunting to help ***"retrieve"*** game like ducks and waterfowl.

As the name indicates, "retrievers" were used to "retrieve" things, but their athletic skills go beyond hunting. For one thing, Retrievers love the water. It is almost instinctive to them and they will not hesitate to get wet.

They thrive on activities that give them *something* to do. It can be a nice game of fetch, some fun at the beach, running around the yard, or racing across an open field.

Although bred as a part of working dog, Golden retrievers are one of the top ten most popular dog breeds today. They are also well known for their participation in conformation shows. Their versatile nature extends beyond dog shows and into the home.

For example, Golden Retrievers are used as guide dogs for the blind and hearing dogs for those who are impaired. Their skills include search and rescue and detection dogs.

They love to play but this does not mean they are not trainable. Retrievers love to learn new things, so training your dog to accept new commands is a breeze!

When it comes to relationships, the Retriever's gentle and patient demeanor makes them an excellent companion for children, and their affectionate nature will endear them to the entire family.

Although exercise is required for this breed, it can enjoy calm indoor activities as well. And, its tranquil nature makes it a delight no matter where you may be.

For these reasons and many more, Golden Retrievers are highly recommended as a loyal and faithful companion. Their steadfast obedient and loyal nature is not only deserving of the title *"man's best friend"* but also… *"Best family friend*!"

A gift just for you!

 **Chapter 1**

An interesting start – Scottish Highlands

Golden retrievers have a very interesting history going back to the Scottish Highlands. During the 19th century, high ranking individuals were busy developing the best dog for hunting parties.

In those days, a man by the name of Sir Dudley Majoribanks, also known as Lord Tweedmouth, wanted the perfect hunting dog. His grand estate was the ideal location to develop the breed he was looking for. So how did Lord Tweedmouth get started?

He bought a yellow retriever named 'Nous' from a cobbler who lived in Brighton, England. The dog was great at swimming and loved living at Lord Tweedmouth's estate.

In the year 1868 Lord Tweedmouth found a partner for Nous. This partner was a Tweed water spaniel named Belle. Soon four beautiful yellow puppies were born. They were affectionately named 'Primrose, Crocus, Ada and Cowslip.'

Belle came from a great line of dogs too! Although this breed is now extinct, she is credited with many of the beautiful qualities including retrieval skills in the modern Golden Retrievers we know today.

But, Lord Tweedmouth's dream for the perfect dog did not stop there. He kept 'Primrose and Cowslip' and mixed them with other breeds over the years. This blending leads us to Culham Kennels. And it was there that one of the first great Golden Retrievers appeared by the name Culham Brass.

It wasn't until the year 1903 in England that the Kennel club accepted the Golden retrievers for registration. However, even before the 1900's in the year 1893, the first Golden Retriever was documented in the

United States. Again Lord Tweedmouth's influence is responsible for this appearance. His son came to America and brought 'Lady' to the Rocking Chair family ranch in Texas.

Although over one hundred years has passed by, the Golden Retriever maintains its well-rounded nature and has become an excellent "all around dog."

To think about: Golden retrievers shed, shed and shed some more! If you have allergies, you need to take this characteristic into account. Why? Because…more than likely you will find hair on your floor, couch, chair, clothes, and everywhere else!

Note of advice: Brushing the coat of your Retriever is a great way to keep the shedding down. You may want to do it a couple times during the week (Occasional or at least two times per week is recommended) to get rid of loose hair. If not, it will fall out or get matted in places you may not necessarily like!

A nice stroll

A dog by any other name...

Golden Retrievers love children and are gentle with them. They are well known as fun loving animals, but when it comes to work time they will work themselves to the ground if necessary. So it is important to take care of this aspect of your dog's nature, and make sure it gets adequate rest.

This breed is active requiring daily exercise, and their playful personality is very obvious outdoors. It is not unusual to see your Golden Retriever "retrieving" things and taking it from one place to another. However, once inside this breed is calm and collected, which makes it a perfect family pet out and in!

Retrievers do not have an aggressive bone in their body. And if you find an exception to this rule, it is considered highly unacceptable. The general disposition of this breed is a calm, affectionate and friendly behavior.

If you decide to teach your Retriever to be a good guard dog, you may give up in despair concluding the effort is a waste of time. More than likely your dog will show strangers into your bedroom with a happy smile! So if you require a guard dog, the Retriever is not for you.

Important note: Like some dog breeds, Golden Retrievers take a long time to mature into adulthood. Usually this maturity may come after three or four years. In some cases this goofy like behavior may last well into old age. You will enjoy their puppy like antics for a few years, which could be quite delightful or give you a bit of a headache!

Strong & Steady

 **Chapter 2**

Now that you know what a Golden Retriever is like and its origins, let us review its features:

In review: Golden Retrievers are beautiful dogs with a loving personality. They are great companions and eager to serve your every need.

When it comes to behavior, their friendly and generous nature will bring a smile to your face and leave you wanting more. Although they require daily exercise, they can be calm indoors making them the perfect family pet.

This gentle nature makes them an ideal companion for children, and they don't mind strangers. They are even friendly with other dogs and cats too.

As a whole, Golden Retrievers are wonderful companions and the perfect family pet.

Best of friends

FUN FACTS FOR KIDS: Did you know there are different types of Golden Retrievers? There is the British type, American type and Canadian type. Would you like to know the difference? Ask your parents or a guardian to help you find out what makes each breed unique!

Want to play?

- ***How much can they weigh?*** The male can weigh approximately 65-75 pounds, and the female can weigh approximately 60-70 pounds. This doesn't mean a Retriever can't weigh more / less than this, but this is the standard weight.

-***How tall can they get?*** A male can reach 23 – 24 inches in height, and a female can get to 21.5 – 22.5 inches in height.

-***What about babies?*** Golden Retrievers litters vary. The female can have between 4 -12 puppies. However, the average size is 8 puppies.

-***How long to they live?*** Lifespan is usually between 10 - 12 years.

-***What about their coat?*** Retrievers have a top coat and an under coat. Both of these are very important to this dog breed. Why? We have learned that Retrievers love water so the top coat is water resistant. The under coat is a dual coat. It keeps the dog cool in summer and warm in winter. The top coat does tend to grow long and wavy, so it should be trimmed.

-*How often do they shed?* Quite a bit! If you suffer from allergies, this is something to consider.

-*What color are they?* Golden Retrievers have beautiful coats in lustrous shades of gold to dark golden colors. This extends to cream tones, pure white and reddish tones. There is also the intriguing color called *Bea Mahogany,* which is called a "redhead."

- *What about their temperament or personality?* As noted Golden Retrievers have an amazing personality. Their high intelligence and cheerful personality are a delightful aspect of their personality. They are also honest and loyal and happy to spend time with you. They also keep a low bark profile. So if you love peace and quiet, this breed is the right one for you!

Golden Retriever next to sea

Caring for your Retriever

Golden Retrievers are not only our pets, but also valued members of our home. Therefore, we want to be sure they get proper care and like most, if not all of us, the right diet and exercise is important.

Let us begin with the right diet:

Gauging how much your dog should eat is a good place to start. If you notice your pet may be getting a little too heavy, cut back on the food intake. If you notice too little weight, then increase the portions of food.

How can you be sure if your dog is being fed correctly? The same principle applies for other breeds, but this general rule of thumb is a nice way to test your animal to see how well you are feeding him.

Try the following test listed on **dogtime.com** at home. Are you ready?

FIRST: Put your thumbs on his spine and run your fingers along the side of the Boxers body.

SECOND: Once there, feel for his ribs beneath the muscle. If you can see them, he needs more food! If you cannot feel them (Too many rolls of fat), you need to put him / her on a diet.

Mealtime

There are lots of choices to feed your Golden Retrievers, so it may be hard to choose the best food on the market. These steps (below) will help you to make an informed and honest decision regarding the best dog food for your beloved pet.

Grrmf.org notes the following recommendations to ensure a happy and healthy pet.

Scratch chemical preservatives: Be on the lookout for ingredients like Ethoxyquin, BHT, BHA, propylene glycol or sodium nitrates in any form. That includes sodium nitrites too! Instead look for natural preservatives such as Rosemary (herbs), and natural Tocopherols.

Expiration date: Be sure to check the expiration date on the bag. You should purchase food months ahead of this date. Why? Moldy food could be a health factor and you never want to feed your dog this kind of food, which can affect its good health. Usually the bag itself is an indicator. Does it look fresh or do you see grease stains somewhere? Stay away from those unsavory looking bags! Ask the store helpers if you are not sure whether the bag is fresh or not.

A bite of meat: Meat ingredient is a great choice, but be sure it is the FIRST ingredient. This can be Turkey, Lamb or Chicken. Do not buy food with Grain as the first ingredient. Why not? Meat protein is what you are looking for. This is the best nutrition for your pet, so search for the meat ingredient as one of the most (if not the most) important in the list. Remember your pet needs animal protein for a beneficial diet.

Avoid animal digest: This is the intestines of other animals! They can contain feet, heads and slaughterhouse waste of other animals. An example as noted at the website is "poultry byproducts."

Sugars and artificial colors: These additives are not healthy or beneficial for your pet so avoid them.

Dog treats: Try to get healthy treats! There are many out there with ingredients that could harm your pet. You could try your hand at making them yourself. Make it a family project and have some fun.

The list could go on and on, but you get the idea! Of course if you have the time to make home cooked food for your pet it would be a great alternative to ensure healthy meals.

The website **Allboxerinfo.com** noted some great tips. Although the website lists another type of dog breed, the same principle applies for your pet.

The recommended meat ingredients among others are:

Lean chicken
Lamb
Veal
Turkey
Fish

Next are the vegetables.

Sweet potatoes
Carrots
Cauliflower
Potatoes
String beans
Sweet peas

Finish off with an excellent multivitamin or supplement (For dogs) and voila! You have a well fed, healthy, and happy pet.

Note: Not all of us have time to do home cooked meals for our pets, and your pet may not be a fan of vegetables! However, if you decide to purchase commercial dog food, take the time to find the healthiest alternative available and the most nutritious supplements for your pet.

Happy and healthy

Exercises

Golden Retrievers do require daily exercise and this can include:

-Breaking a sweat

Retrievers need exercise so you can jog, run or walk briskly to get their blood flowing. (Note: This is a daily requirement, so if you unable to meet this type of demand on your time, a Retriever may not be the ideal pet for you – If you still want one but need to find other ways to keep the pet occupied, talk to a dog trainer or reputable veterinarian for their advice.)

-Swimming

Golden Retrievers love water, so this is an excellent way for your pet to get the exercise it needs. They also love to 'retrieve' things, so enjoy a game of throw ball, stick or whatever else comes to mind!

-Running

Try to stay away from really hard surfaces. An open field (park area or similar site) is better for it is low impact on the frame of your pet. This will help their joints and feet to keep in tip top shape.

Golden Retrievers are gentle and kind

Living with the family

Children will love having a Golden Retriever as a pet. They are great playmates and will interact well with other family pets. Of course to interact with family pets (Like other dogs and cats), there is a degree of socialization required, but it will not be too difficult.

Retrievers enjoy the companionship of their human family, and they thrive on loving affection. So be sure to include him / her in your family activities. It is important to note a Retriever's loving affection will put him / her underfoot! So if you do not wish to have the dog constantly at your side, you will have to find other creative ways to occupy their time.

🐾 Chapter 3

Come out and play with me!

Keeping it effective

Michele Welton from the website '*your pure bread puppy*' recommends the following training method. (This applies to all dog breeds and not just Golden Retrievers)

Try **RESPECT TRAINING**. This is where you actually teach your pet to learn from **POSITIVE** and **NEGATIVE** consequences.

As a human we also learn from these same principles. For example: If we do something for someone and they say thank you, we may do it again. And yet if we forget to take out the garbage, and Daddy blows his top, more than likely we will not do it again. (At least we hope!)

Dogs, and in this case Retrievers, learn in the same way. If our pet does something great we can reward it with smiles, hugs, laughs, kisses, games, treats, and whatever other happy outcome you will like. Trust me when I say Retrievers will LOVE it!

On the other hand, if our pet does something we do not like we can transmit that with our voice, our look or use the leash or collar. It is important to note you will not hit, kick or otherwise abuse the animal. A simple tug with a firm voice is usually enough for the animal to figure out something is off.

This dignifies the dog and teaches it both respect and appreciation for boundaries. With loving attention and care, you can have a happy, obedient pet and a happy home.

When it comes specifically to Golden Retrievers, Michelle notes the following:

Teach your dog words and *what* the word actually means! Sound complicated? Think about it this way.

Educate your pet to know what you are saying and thinking and they will respond in kind. Dogs, and in this case Retrievers, love to know what they should and what they shouldn't do. They thrive on this type of relationship and will respect you as the "pack leader" if you assert this type of authority.

For example; if you tell your pet to get the walking rope, help your pet to not only understand that you *want* the rope, but also that you *need* him to bring it to you!

If you are unsure how to do this, talk to a reputable veterinarian or look up the training methods online.

So, what else can we learn about Retrievers? Check out some other details you may like to know.

- Golden Retrievers are not very good guard dogs. Their gentle nature and kind disposition means they are friendly even to strangers. So if you are looking for good protection at home, this dog may not be ideal. And yet their calm nature is so appealing, you might forget about their poor guarding skills, and get one anyway!

- They can sit quietly for hours if needed, and conceal themselves well in a hunting blind. If you have never heard of the term, a hunting blind is a device used by hunters to avoid the risk of detection.

- Golden Retrievers love to eat food, so ensure a proper and healthy diet by measuring the portions of food required. If not, your pet will get overweight and this could lead to serious health problems.

- Golden Retrievers thrive on your loving affection. So do not leave them alone in the backyard and forget all about them!

- Golden Retrievers are boisterous and playful. Their happy spirit could accidentally knock over a child in their efforts to show loving attention. It is important to note this action is not intentional. It is simply a reflection of their happiness to be around you. And soon, their devotion and sincere affection will have you forgetting about their slight imperfections!

- **<u>Caution:</u>** Many people breed Golden Retrievers only for money, so it is important to get your dog from a reputable breeder. If you are not sure what to do or where to go, talk to your veterinarian or a trusted friend to make the best possible choice!

So much fun

FUN FACTS FOR KIDS: Britain's Golden Retriever Club celebrated their 100th year anniversary by visiting an old estate in Scotland. They invited hundreds of dogs and their owners to a place called Guisachan Estate. Many dog owners came from far away, even as far as Australia, to attend. Do you know why they went there? Ask your parents or a guardian's permission to look it up online!

 **Conclusion**

Best family friend

In conclusion:

Golden Retrievers are a beautiful addition to your family home and the perfect family pet. They are also versatile, easy to train, and eager to please you.

Retrievers are amazing with children and ever patient and caring with them. On occasion, they may get a little excited and knock someone over, but they don't really mean it. This action only reflects the overwhelming happiness they feel to be a part of your life.

Their natural ability is reflected not only in their stride, but also their loving Golden smile. It is true that being a watchdog is not for them, so don't expect it! However, their affections and faithful nature outshines any perceived flaws.

More than any other breed, Golden Retrievers are everyone's best friend! If you decide to make this breed a part of your family home, you could not make a better choice than a devoted, outgoing, and charming pet!

Author Bio

K. Bennett is a native from the Island of Roatan, North of Honduras. She loves to write about many different subjects, but writing for children is special to her heart.

Some of her favorite pastimes are reading, traveling and discovering new things. These activities help to fuel her imagination and act like a canvas for more stories.

She also loves fantasy elements like hidden worlds and faraway lands. Basically anything that gets her imagination soaring to new heights!

Her writing credits include local newspaper articles, a writing blog at Wordpress.com and other online stories. It also includes nonfiction books, children books online, and two novellas listed on Amazon.com

Our books are available at

1. Amazon.com
2. Barnes and Noble
3. Itunes
4. Kobo
5. Smashwords
6. Google Play Books

This book is published by

JD-Biz Corp

P O Box 374

Mendon, Utah 84325

http://www.jd-biz.com/

CPSIA information can be obtained
at www.ICGtesting.com
Printed in the USA
LVHW071618180520
655935LV00021B/1279